WARDROBE FAVORITES

Lisa J. Ellis

As a knitter, you know that creating a fine garment is a wonderful experience—it's just so uplifting to know that the perfect sweater truly exists, and that you made it yourself! These designs by Lisa J. Ellis offer you six new options for getting that lovely creative high.

Like many knitters, Lisa originally learned the skill from her mother. While a student in college, Lisa encountered a European method for knitting fit-as-you-go garments without the use of written instructions. It was an experience that helped her grow as a designer, and it continues to inspire her work. These days, Lisa is an avid gardener, cook, and mother of two girls. She is also a knitting instructor who teaches in several yarn shops in the Greater Seattle/Tacoma area.

Lisa designed the cardigans, pullovers, bolero, and shell in this collection to be wardrobe builders you'll rely on, while the clear instructions will make creating them a true pleasure.

LEISURE ARTS, INC.
Maumelle, Arkansas

Feminine Frills

INTERMEDIATE

This sweater is worked in a Twisted Stockinette Stitch with a loose fit at the hips and decreases at the waistline for a fitted bodice. The ruffles add a sweetly feminine touch.

Size	Finished Chest Measurement	
32	32"	(81.5 cm)
34	33 1/2"	(85 cm)
36	35 1/2"	(90 cm)
38	38"	(96.5 cm)
40	40"	(101.5 cm)
42	42 1/2"	(108 cm)

Size Note: Instructions are written with sizes 32, 34, and 36 in the first set of braces { } and sizes 38, 40, and 42 in the second set of braces. Instructions will be easier to read if you circle all the numbers pertaining to your size. If only one number is given, it applies to all sizes.

MATERIALS

MEDIUM 4

Medium Weight Yarn
[3.5 ounces, 163 yards
(100 grams, 149 meters) per skein]:
{4-5-5} {6-6-7} skeins
Straight knitting needles, size 8 (5 mm) **or** size needed for gauge
24" (61 cm) Circular knitting needles, sizes 8 (5 mm) **and** 10 (6 mm)
Yarn needle

GAUGE: With smaller size needles,
in Twisted Stockinette Stitch,
18 sts and 24 rows = 4" (10 cm)

STITCH GUIDE

TWISTED RIBBING

★ K1 tbl ***(Fig. 1, page 31)***, P1; repeat from ★ for ribbing.

TWISTED STOCKINETTE STITCH

Right Side Rows: Knit each stitch working through back loop only ***(Fig. 1, page 31)***.

Wrong Side Rows: Purl across.

BACK

With smaller size straight needles, cast on {82-86-90} {96-100-106} sts.

Work in Twisted Ribbing for 1" (2.5 cm).

Work in Twisted Stockinette Stitch until piece measures approximately 5" (12.5 cm) from cast on edge, ending by working a **purl** row.

WAISTLINE SHAPING

Row 1 (Decrease row)**:** K1 tbl, SSK ***(Figs. 8a-c, page 33)***, knit tbl across to last 3 sts, K2 tog ***(Fig. 7, page 33)***, K1 tbl: {80-84-88}{94-98-104} sts.

Continue to decrease one stitch at each edge in same manner, every sixth row, 3 times **more**: {74-78-82}{88-92-98} sts.

Work even until piece measures approximately {12-12-12}{12-12 1/2-12 1/2}"/{30.5-30.5-30.5} {30.5-32-32} cm from cast on edge, ending by working a **purl** row.

Instructions continued on page 4.

ARMHOLE SHAPING

Rows 1 and 2: Bind off {5-5-5}{5-6-6} sts, work across: {64-68-72}{78-80-86} sts.

Row 3 (Decrease row)**:** K1 tbl, SSK, knit tbl across to last 3 sts, K2 tog, K1 tbl: {62-66-70}{76-78-84} sts.

Continue to decrease one stitch at **each** edge in same manner, every other row, {4-4-3}{4-4-5} times **more**: {54-58-64}{68-70-74} sts.

Work even until Armholes measure approximately {7-7½-8}{8½-9-9½}"/{18-19-20.5}{21.5-23-24} cm, ending by working a **purl** row.

SHOULDER SHAPING

Rows 1-4: Bind off {4-5-6}(6-6-7} sts, work across: {38-38-40}{44-46-46} sts.

Rows 5 and 6: Bind off {5-4-5}(6-7-6} sts, work across: {28-30-30}{32-32-34} sts.

Bind off remaining sts.

FRONT

Work same as Back until Armholes measure approximately {3½-3½-4}{4-4-4}"/{9-9-10}{10-10-10} cm, ending by working a **purl** row: {54-58-64}{68-70-74} sts.

Note: Sweater includes two edge stitches.

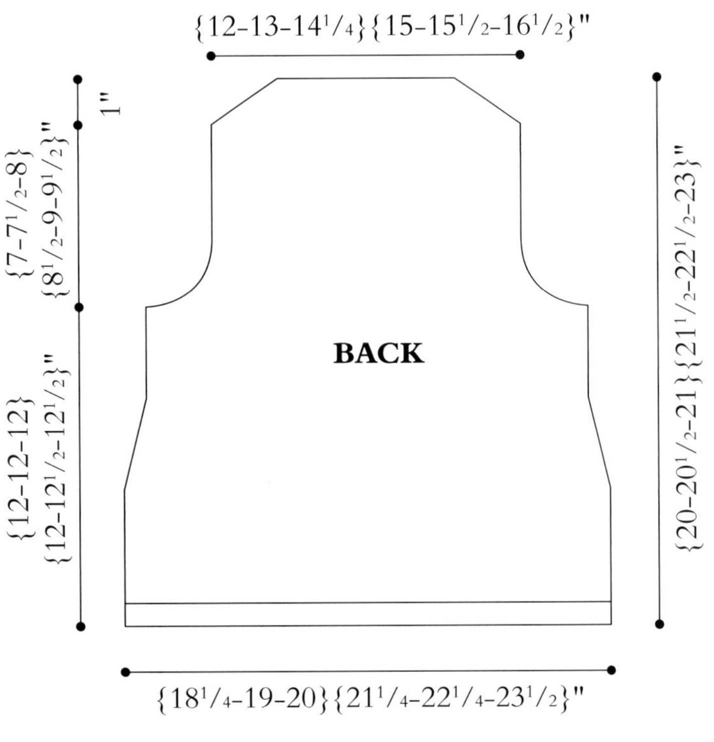

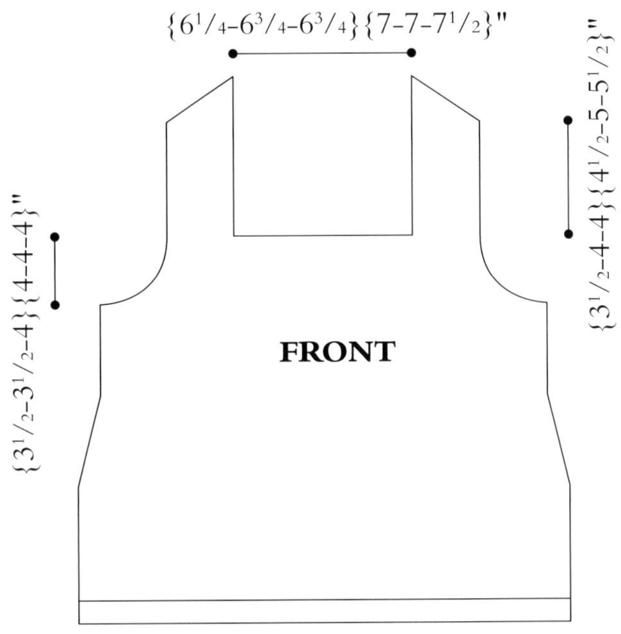

NECK SHAPING

Both sides of Neck are worked at the same time using separate yarn for **each** side. Maintain established pattern throughout.

Note: It takes two stitches to bind off the first stitch.

Row 1: Work across {13-14-17}{18-19-20} sts, bind off center {28-30-30}{32-32-34} sts; with second yarn, work across: {13-14-17}{18-19-20} sts **each** side.

Work even until Front measures same as Back to Shoulder Shaping, ending by working a **purl** row.

SHOULDER SHAPING

Rows 1-4: Bind off {4-5-6}(6-6-7} sts, work across; with second yarn, work across: {5-4-5}(6-7-6} sts **each** side.

Row 5: Bind off remaining sts on first side; with second yarn, work across.

Bind off remaining sts.

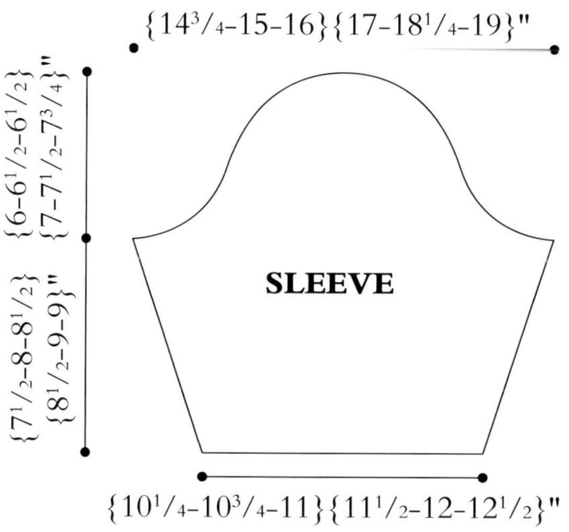

SLEEVE (Make 2)

With smaller size straight needles, cast on {46-48-50}{52-54-56} sts.

Work in Twisted Stockinette Stitch increasing one stitch at **each** edge ***(Figs. 4a & b, page 32)***, every other row, {0-0-0}{2-4-6} times ***(see Zeros, page 30)***; then increase every fourth row, {10-10-11}{10-10-9} times: {66-68-72}{76-82-86} sts.

Work even until Sleeve measures approximately {7$^1/_2$-8-8$^1/_2$}{8$^1/_2$-9-9}"/{19-20.5-21.5}{21.5-23-23} cm from cast on edge, ending by working a **purl** row.

CAP SHAPING

Rows 1 and 2: Bind off {5-5-5}{5-6-6} sts, work across: {56-58-62}{66-70-74} sts.

Row 3 (Decrease row)**:** K1 tbl, SSK, knit tbl across to last 3 sts, K2 tog, K1 tbl: {54-56-60}{64-68-72} sts.

Continue to decrease one stitch at **each** edge in same manner, every other row, {13-16-16}{18-19-19} times **more**; then decrease every row, {4-2-2}{2-2-4} times: {20-20-24}{24-26-26} sts.

Next 4 Rows: Bind off {2-2-3}{3-3-3} sts, work across: {12-12-12}{12-14-14} sts.

Bind off remaining sts.

Instructions continued on page 6.

SLEEVE RUFFLE

With **right** side facing and using smaller size straight needles, pick up {46-48-50}{52-54-56} sts across cast on edge of Sleeve ***(Fig. 14b, page 35)***; cut yarn.

Set aside for 3-needle bind off to join Ruffle.

With larger size needle, cast on {92-96-100}{104-108-112} sts.

Work in Twisted Stockinette Stitch for 2" (5 cm), ending by working a **purl** row.

Decrease Row: K2 tog across: (46-48-50}{52-54-56} sts.

Next Row: Purl across.

Placing Ruffle and Sleeve with **right** sides together and using larger size needle, join pieces together using the 3-needle bind off method ***(Fig. 13, page 34)***.

FINISHING

Sew left shoulder seam.

NECK RUFFLE

With **right** side facing and using smaller size circular needle, pick up {28-30-30}{32-32-34} sts across Back Neck edge ***(Fig. 14a, page 35)***, pick up {20-22-22}{24-26-28} sts evenly spaced along left Front Neck edge and one st in corner, pick up {28-30-30}{32-32-34} sts across bound off sts, pick up one st in corner and {20-22-22}{24-26-28} sts evenly spaced along right Front Neck edge; cut yarn: {98-106-106}{114-118-126} sts.

Set aside for 3-needle bind off to join Ruffle.

With larger size needle, cast on {196-212-212}{228-236-252} sts.

Work in Twisted Stockinette Stitch for 2" (5 cm), ending by working a **purl** row.

Decrease Row: K2 tog across: {98-106-106}{114-118-126} sts.

Next Row: Purl across.

Placing **right** side of Ruffle to **wrong** side of Sweater and using larger size needle, join pieces together using the 3-needle bind-off method.

Sew remaining shoulder seam.

Weave ends of Ruffle together ***(Fig. 15, page 35)***.

Fold Ruffle to **right** side and tack down at each shoulder.

Sew Sleeves to sweater, placing center of Sleeve Cap at shoulder seam and matching bound off sts at underarm.

Weave underarm and side in one continuous seam.

just enough

INTERMEDIATE

This cardigan will make a dependable addition to any wardrobe. The sleeve length goes nicely with a favorite bracelet. The cropped length is very stylish, but should a longer version be desired, simply add the additional inches prior to the armhole shaping. Additional length may also require additional yardage.

Size	Finished Chest Measurement	
32	33½"	(85 cm)
34	36½"	(92.5 cm)
36	38"	(96.5 cm)
38	41"	(104 cm)
40	42½"	(108 cm)
42	45"	(114.5 cm)

Size Note: Instructions are written with sizes 32, 34, and 36 in the first set of braces { } and sizes 38, 40, and 42 in the second set of braces. Instructions will be easier to read if you circle all the numbers pertaining to your size. If only one number is given, it applies to all sizes.

MATERIALS

MEDIUM 4

Medium Weight Yarn
[3.5 ounces, 132 yards (100 grams, 121 meters) per hank]:
{6-7-7}{8-8-9} hanks
Straight knitting needles, size 9 (5.5 mm) **or** size needed for gauge
29" (73.5 cm) Circular knitting needle, size 9 (5.5 mm)
Stitch holders - 3
Split-ring markers
Cable needle
2" (5 cm) Button
Yarn needle

GAUGE: In Flying Birds Pattern,
18 sts and 22 rows = 4" (10 cm)

Gauge Swatch: 6¼"w x 4"h (16 cm x 10 cm)
Cast on 28 sts.
Work 22 rows in Flying Birds Pattern.
Bind off all sts.

STITCH GUIDE

BACK CABLE (uses next 3 sts)
Slip next 2 sts onto cable needle and hold in **back** of work, K1 from left needle, K2 from cable needle.

FRONT CABLE (uses next 3 sts)
Slip next st onto cable needle and hold in **front** of work, K2 from left needle, K1 from cable needle.

FLYING BIRDS PATTERN (multiple of 10 plus 8 sts)

Row 1: (Right side)**:** Knit across.
Row 2: Purl across.
Row 3: K8, (slip 2 sts as if to **purl**, K8) across.
Row 4: P8, (slip 2 sts as if to **purl**, P8) across.
Row 5: K6, work back cable, work front cable, (K4, work back cable, work front cable) across to last 6 sts, K6.
Row 6: Purl across.
Row 7: Knit across.
Row 8: Purl across.
Row 9: K3, slip 2 sts as if to **purl**, (K8, slip 2 sts as if to **purl**) across to last 3 sts, K3.
Row 10: P3, slip 2 sts as if to **purl**, (P8, slip 2 sts as if to **purl**) across to last 3 sts, P3.
Row 11: K1, work back cable, work front cable, (K4, work back cable, work front cable) across to last st, K1.
Row 12: Purl across.
Repeat Rows 1-12 for pattern.

Instructions continued on page 8.

BACK

RIBBING

Cast on {78-84-88}{94-98-104} sts.

Work in K1, P1 ribbing for 1" (2.5 cm).

BODY

For sizes 34, 38, and 42, place first marker after third stitch ***(see Markers, page 30)***, and second marker before last 3 stitches. Work the Flying Birds Pattern between the markers and edge stitches in Stockinette Stitch. For the remaining three sizes, the entire row is worked in Flying Birds Pattern.

Work in Flying Birds Pattern until Back measures approximately {9-9-9}{$9^{1}/_{2}$-$9^{1}/_{2}$-10}"/{23-23-23}{24-24-25.5} cm from cast on edge, ending by working a **wrong** side row.

ARMHOLE SHAPING

Rows 1 and 2: Bind off {2-2-2}{4-5-5} sts, work across in pattern: {74-80-84}{86-88-94} sts.

Work even until Armholes measure approximately {$8^{1}/_{4}$-$8^{1}/_{2}$-$8^{3}/_{4}$}{9-$9^{1}/_{4}$-$9^{1}/_{2}$}"/{21-21.5-22}{23-23.5-24} cm, ending by working a **wrong** side row.

Slip first {23-26-27}{27-28-30} sts onto st holder for right shoulder 3-needle bind off; slip next {28-28-30}{32-32-34} sts onto second st holder for neck; slip remaining {23-26-27}{27-28-30} sts onto third st holder for left shoulder 3-needle bind off; cut yarn.

LEFT FRONT

RIBBING

Cast on {38-42-44}{46-48-52} sts.

Work in K1, P1 ribbing for 1" (2.5 cm).

BODY

For sizes 34, 36, 38, and 42, place first marker after {0-2-3}{4-0-2} stitches ***(see Zeros, page 30)***, and second marker before last {0-2-3}{4-0-2} stitches. Work the Flying Birds Pattern between the markers and edge stitches in Stockinette Stitch. For remaining two sizes, the entire row is worked in Flying Birds Pattern.

Work in Flying Birds Pattern until Left Front measures approximately {8-8-$8^{1}/_{2}$}{9-9-$9^{1}/_{2}$}"/{20.5-20.5-21.5}{23-23-24} cm from cast on edge, ending by working a **wrong** side row.

NECK SHAPING

Maintain established pattern throughout.

Row 1 (Decrease row)**:** Work across to last 3 sts, K2 tog ***(Fig. 7, page 33)***, K1: {37-41-43}{45-47-51} sts.

Continue to decrease one stitch at neck edge in same manner, every other row, {2-3-6}{5-4-8} times **more**; then decrease every fourth row, {10-10-8}{9-10-8} times AND AT THE SAME TIME, when Left Front measures same as Back to Armhole Shaping, bind off {2-2-2}{4-5-5} sts at Armhole edge: {23-26-27}{27-28-30} sts.

Work even until Left Front measures same as Back, ending by working a **right** side row.

Slip Back left shoulder sts onto straight needle.

Placing **right** sides together and using a circular needle, join Left Front to Back at shoulder using the 3-needle bind off method ***(Fig. 13, page 34)***.

Instructions continued on page 10.

RIGHT FRONT

Work same as Left Front to Neck Shaping.

NECK SHAPING

Maintain established pattern throughout.

Row 1 (Decrease row)**:** K1, SSK ***(Figs. 8a-c, page 33)***, work across: {37-41-43}{45-47-51} sts.

Continue to decrease one stitch at neck edge in same manner, every other row, {2-3-6}{5-4-8} times **more**; then decrease every fourth row, {10-10-8}{9-10-8} times AND AT THE SAME TIME, when Right Front measures same as Back to Armhole Shaping, bind off {2-2-2}{4-5-5} sts at Armhole edge: {23-26-27}{27-28-30} sts.

Work even until Right Front measures same as Back, ending by working a **right** side row.

Slip Back right shoulder sts onto straight needle.

Placing **right** sides together and using circular needle, join Right Front to Back at shoulder using the 3-needle bind off method.

SLEEVE (Make 2)

RIBBING

Cast on {48-48-48}{48-48-52} sts.

Work K1, P1 ribbing for 1" (2.5 cm).

BODY

For size 42, place first marker after second stitch and second marker before last two stitches. Work the Flying Birds Pattern between the markers and edge stitcches in Stockinette Stitch.

Note: Cardigan includes two edge stitches

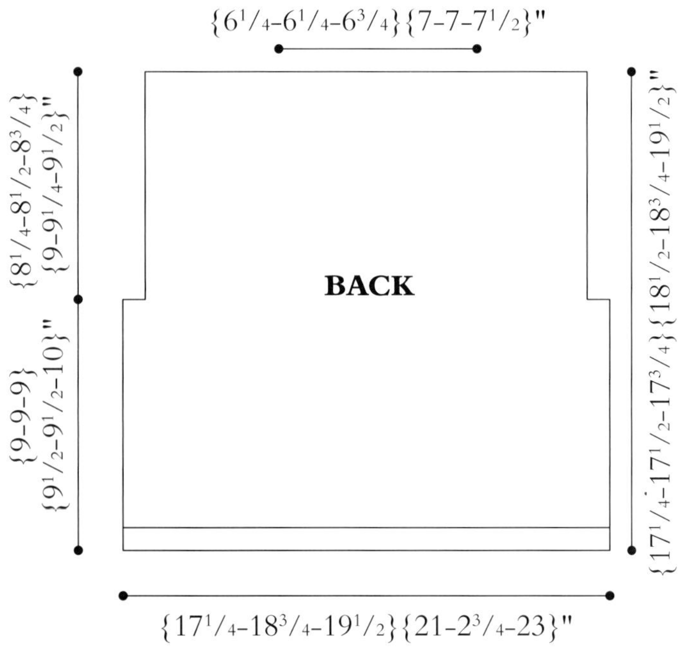

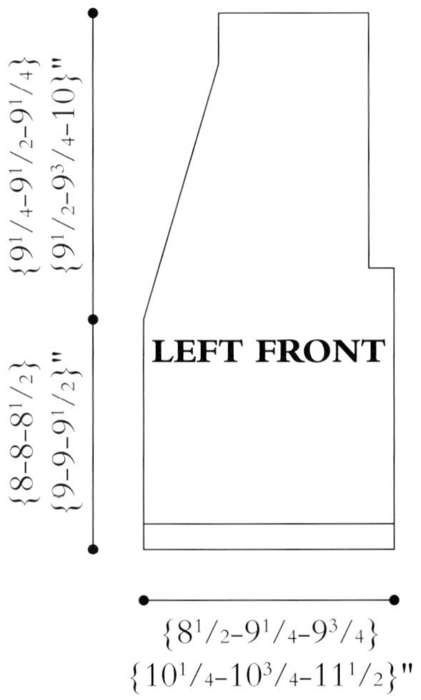

Work in Flying Birds Pattern, increasing one stitch at **each** edge ***(Figs. 4a & b, page 32)***, every fourth row, {6-8-9}{11-16-11} times, working new stitches in pattern; then increase every sixth row, {7-6-6}{5-2-6} times: {74-76-78}{80-84-86} sts.

Work even until Sleeve measures approximately {14-14 1/2-15}{15 1/2-16-16 1/2}"/{35.5-37-38}{39.5-40.5-42} cm from cast on edge, ending by working a **wrong** side row.

Bind off remaining sts.

FINISHING

Sew Sleeves to sweater, placing center of Sleeve at shoulder seam.

Weave underarm and side in one continuous seam ***(Fig. 15, page 35)***.

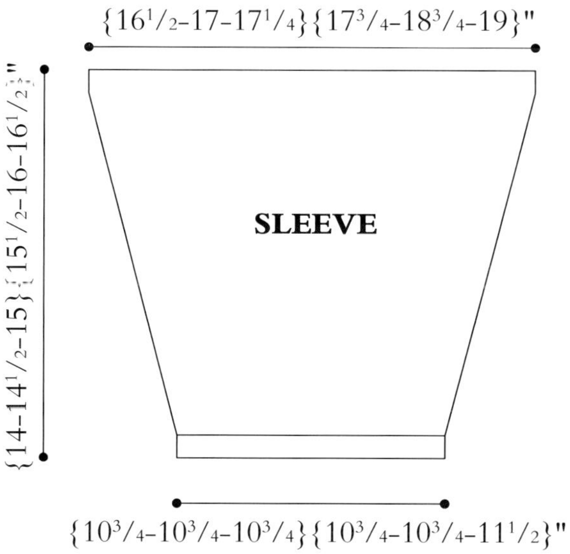

BAND

With **right** side facing and using circular needle, pick up {40-40-42}{46-46-48} sts evenly spaced across Right Front edge to beginning of Neck Shaping ***(Figs. 14a & b, page 35)***, place marker for buttonhole, pick up {46-48-46}{48-50-50} sts evenly spaced along neck edge, slip {28-28-30}{32-32-34} sts from Back neck st holder onto empty needle and knit across, pick up {46-48-46}{48-50-50} sts evenly spaced along Left Front neck edge to end of Neck Shaping, pick up {40-40-42}{46-46-48} sts evenly spaced along Left Front: {200-204-206}{220-224-230} sts.

Rows 1 and 2: (K1, P1) across.

Note: If a buttonhole is not desired, a sweater pin or large snap would also work nicely. Repeat Rows 1 and 2 once more in place of working Rows 3 and 4.

Row 3 (Buttonhole Row)**:** Work across in established ribbing to marker, bind off 5 sts, work across.

Row 4: Work across to bound off sts, **turn**; add on 5 sts ***(Figs. 2a & b, page 31)***, **turn**; work across.

Bind off all sts in pattern.

Using yarn, sew button to Left Front opposite buttonhole.

If desired, sew around buttonhole for reinforcement.

light lace-up

EASY

This shell is worked in the round, eliminating side seams. It is close-fitting and flairs slightly at the hip with decreases at the waistline. If you desire a looser fit, knit the next larger size.

Size	Finished Bust Measurement	
30	30$^1/_2$"	(77.5 cm)
32	32"	(81.5 cm)
34	34"	(86.5 cm)
36	36"	(91.5 cm)
38	38"	(96.5 cm)
40	40"	(101.5 cm)

Size Note: Instructions are written with sizes 30, 32, and 34 in the first set of braces { } and sizes 36, 38, and 40 in the second set of braces. Instructions will be easier to read if you circle all the numbers pertaining to your size. If only one number is given, it applies to all sizes.

MATERIALS

Light Weight Yarn
[2.5 ounces, 168 yards
(70 grams, 154 meters) per skein]:
Pink - {2-3-3}{3-3-3} skeins
Brown - {2-3-3}{3-3-3} skeins
Bulky Weight Ribbon Yarn
[1.75 ounces, 110 yards
(50 grams, 100 meters) per ball]:
1 ball or approximately 3 yards (2.75 meters)
24" (61 cm) Circular knitting needle, size 5 (3.75 mm) **or** size needed for gauge
16" (40.5 cm) **and** 21" (53.5 cm) Circular knitting needles, size 4 (3.5 mm)
Markers - 2
Stitch holders - 2
Tapestry needle
Yarn needle

GAUGE: With larger size needle,
in Stockinette Stitch,
23 sts and 28 rows/rnds = 4" (10 cm)

BODY

With larger size needle and Pink, cast on {188-196-208}{220-232-244} sts; place marker to indicate the beginning of the round ***(see Markers, page 30)***.

Taking care not to twist the cast on sts, purl one round.

Knit each round until Body measures approximately {3$^1/_2$-3$^1/_2$-4}{4-4$^1/_2$-4$^1/_2$}"/{9-9-10}{10-11.5-11.5} cm from cast on edge.

WAISTLINE SHAPING

Rnd 1 (Decrease rnd)**:** K1, SSK ***(Figs. 8a-c, page 33)***, knit {88-92-98}{104-110-116} sts, K2 tog ***(Fig. 7, page 33)***, K1, place a different color marker to indicate side, K1, SSK, knit across to last 3 sts, K2 tog, K1: {184-192-204}{216-228-240} sts.

Rnds 2-7: Knit around.

Rnd 8 (Decrease rnd)**:** K1, SSK, knit across to within 3 sts of marker, K2 tog, K2, SSK, knit across to last 3 sts, K2 tog, K1: {180-188-200}{212-224-236} sts.

Instructions continued on page 14.

Rnds 9-15: Repeat Rnds 2-8: {176-184-196}{208-220-232} sts.

Knit each round until Body measures approximately 10" (25.5 cm) from cast on edge.

First Eyelet Rnd: ★YO ***(Fig. 3a, page 32)***, K2 tog; repeat from ★ around; cut Pink.

Second Eyelet Rnd: With Brown, (K2 tog, YO) around.

Knit each round until Body measures approximately {13$^1/_2$-13$^1/_2$-14}{14-14$^1/_2$-14$^1/_2$}"/{34.5-34.5-35.5}{35.5-37-37} cm from cast on edge.

BACK

ARMHOLE SHAPING

Note: Back and Front are now worked separately in rows.

Row 1: Bind off {4-4-5}{5-6-6} sts, knit across to next marker; slip remaining {88-92-98}{104-110-116} sts onto a st holder (Front): {84-88-93}{99-104-110} sts.

Row 2: Bind off {4-4-5}{5-6-6} sts, purl across: {80-84-88}{94-98-104} sts.

Row 3 (Decrease row)**:** K1, SSK, knit across to last 3 sts, K2 tog, K1: {78-82-86}{92-96-102} sts.

Row 4: Purl across.

Row 5 (Decrease row)**:** K1, SSK, knit across to last 3 sts, K2 tog, K1: {76-80-84}{90-94-100} sts.

Repeat Rows 4 and 5, {0-1-2}{3-3-4} time(s) ***(see Zeros, page 30)***: {76-78-80}{84-88-92} sts.

Work even until Armholes measure approximately {8-8-8}{8$^1/_2$-8$^1/_2$-9}"/{20.5-20.5-20.5}{21.5-21.5-23} cm, ending by working a **purl** row.

SHOULDER SHAPING

Rows 1-4: Bind off {7-7-8}{8-9-9} sts, work across: {48-50-48}{52-52-56} sts.

Rows 5 and 6: Bind off {8-8-7}{8-8-9} sts, work across: {32-34-34}{36-36-38} sts.

Slip remaining sts onto st holder; cut yarn.

FRONT

ARMHOLE & NECK SHAPING

With **right** side facing, slip sts from st holder onto larger size needle.

Rows 1 and 2: Using Brown, bind off {4-4-5}{5-6-6} sts, work across: {80-84-88}{94-98-104} sts.

Row 3 (Decrease row)**:** K1, SSK, knit across to last 3 sts, K2 tog, K1: {78-82-86}{92-96-102} sts.

Note: Dashes indicate continuous rounds.

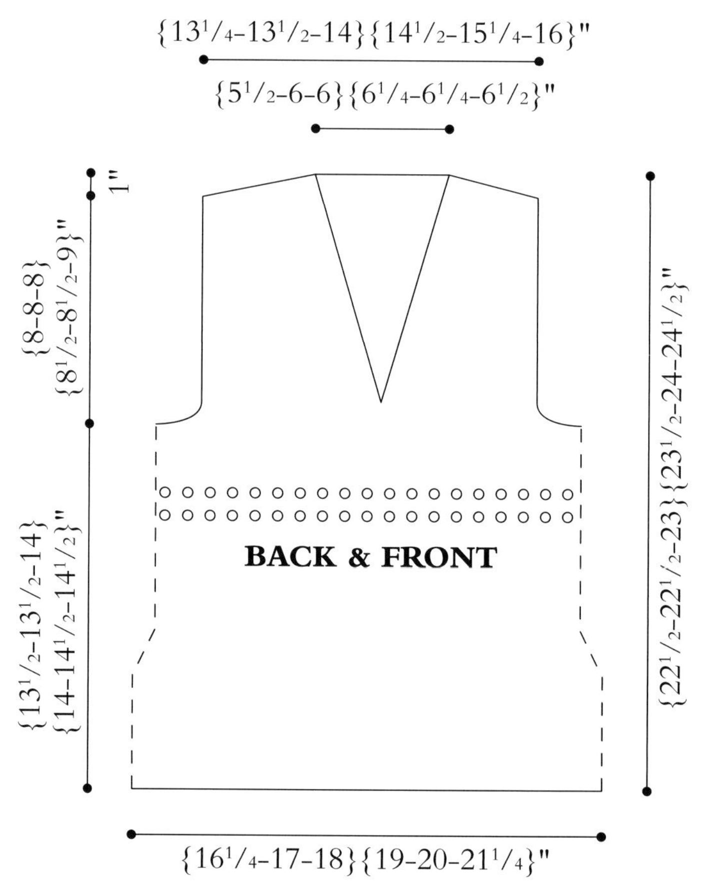

Both sides of Neck are worked at the same time, using separate yarn for **each** side.

Row 4: Purl {39-41-43}{46-48-51} sts; with second yarn, purl across: {39-41-43}{46-48-51} sts **each** side.

Row 5 (Decrease row)**:** K1, SSK, knit across to within 3 sts of Neck edge, K2 tog, K1; with second yarn, K1, SSK, knit across to last 3 sts, K2 tog, K1: {37-39-41}{44-46-49} sts **each** side.

Row 6: Purl across; with second yarn, purl across.

Repeat Rows 5 and 6, {0-1-2}{3-3-4} time(s): {37-37-37}{38-40-41} sts **each** side.

Neck Decrease Row: Knit across to within 3 sts of Neck edge, K2 tog, K1: with second yarn, K1, SSK, knit across: {36-36-36}{37-39-40} sts **each** side.

Continue to decrease one stitch at **each** Neck edge, every other row, {9-10-9}{8-8-8} times **more**; then decrease every fourth row, {5-4-4}{5-5-5} times: {22-22-23}{24-26-27} sts **each** side.

Work even until Front measures same as Back to Shoulder Shaping, ending by working a **purl** row.

SHOULDER SHAPING

Rows 1-4: Bind off {7-7-8}{8-9-9} sts, work across; with second yarn, work across: {8-8-7}{8-8-9} sts **each** side.

Row 5: Bind off remaining sts on first side; with second yarn, work across.

Bind off remaining sts.

FINISHING

Sew shoulder seams.

ARMHOLE EDGING

With **right** side facing, using smaller size 16" (40.5 cm) circular needle and Brown, pick up {92-92-92}{96-96-102} sts evenly spaced around armhole edge ***(Figs. 14a & b, page 35)***; place marker to indicate the beginning of the round.

Rnds 1-3: Knit around.

Rnd 4 (Turning ridge)**:** Purl around.

Rnds 5 and 6: Knit around.

Bind off all sts **loosely** in knit.

Fold Armhole Edging along turning ridge to **wrong** side; using tapestry needle, sew bound off edge in place.

NECK EDGING

With **right** side facing, using smaller size 21" (53.5 cm) circular needle and Brown, pick up {46-46-46}{48-48-50} sts evenly spaced along left Front Neck edge, place marker for center, pick up {46-46-46}{48-48-50} sts along right Front Neck edge, slip {32-34-34}{36-36-38} sts from Back st holder onto second end of circular needle and knit across; place marker to indicate the beginning of the round: {124-126-126}{132-132-138} sts.

Rnds 1-3: Knit across to within 2 sts of center marker, K2 tog, SSK, knit around: {118-120-120}{126-126-132} sts.

Rnd 4 (Turning ridge)**:** Purl around.

Rnds 5-7: Knit around.

Bind off all sts **loosely** in **knit**.

Fold Neck Edging along turning ridge to **wrong** side; using tapestry needle, sew bound off edge in place.

Cut 2 pieces of ribbon yarn approximately $1^1/_2$ yards long or desired length. Using yarn needle and beginning at center Front, weave ribbon yarn through first Eyelet Row. Weave second length through second Eyelet Row. Holding both ribbons together, tie ends in a bow.

plenty of zip

INTERMEDIATE

This classically styled pattern has the look of a true cable, but is actually formed using a decrease and a yarn over. You'll reach for this one time and again!

Size	Finished Chest Measurement	
32	33"	(84 cm)
34	35"	(89 cm)
36	36 1/2"	(92.5 cm)
38	38"	(96.5 cm)
40	41 1/2"	(105.5 cm)
42	43"	(109 cm)

Size Note: Instructions are written with sizes 32, 34, and 36 in the first set of braces { } and sizes 38, 40, and 42 in the second set of braces. Instructions will be easier to read if you circle all the numbers pertaining to your size. If only one number is given, it applies to all sizes.

MATERIALS

MEDIUM 4

Medium Weight Wool Yarn
[3.5 ounces, 223 yards
(100 grams, 205 meters) per skein]:
{6-6-7}{7-8-8} skeins

Straight knitting needles, size 7 (4.5 mm) **or** size needed for gauge

Note: You will need a third needle to work the 3-needle bind off. One size larger than needles used to achieve gauge will work best.

Stitch holders - 3

Yarn needle

Sewing needle and thread

Separating zipper - {18-20-20}{20-22-22}"/ {45.5-51-51}{51-56-56} cm

This pattern shows best when slightly stretched. For best results, use a wool yarn so that it can easily be stretched and steam blocked.

GAUGE: In Reverse Stockinette Stitch,
20 sts and 26 rows = 4" (10 cm)
3 repeats (15 sts) = 2 1/2" (6.25 cm) stretched

BACK

RIBBING

Cast on {102-107-112}{117-127-132} sts.

Work in K1, P1 ribbing for 2" (5 cm).

BODY

Row 1 (Right side)**:** P2, ★ [slip 1 as if to **knit**, K2, PSSO ***(Fig. 10, page 33)***], P2; repeat from ★ across.

Note: You will have one less stitch for every repeat worked. The stitch count will be restored after working the next row.

Row 2: K2, ★ P1, YO ***(Fig. 3b, page 32)***, P1, K2; repeat from ★ across.

Row 3: P2, (K3, P2) across.

Row 4: K2, (P3, K2) across.

Repeat Rows 1-4 for pattern until Back measures approximately {12 1/2-12 1/2-13}{13 1/2-14-14}"/ {32-32-33}{34.5-35.5-35.5} cm from cast on edge, ending by working a **wrong** side row.

Instructions continued on page 18.

ARMHOLE SHAPING

Maintain established pattern throughout.

Rows 1 and 2: Bind off 5 sts, work across: {92-97-102}{107-117-122} sts.

Work even until Armholes measure approximately {8-8$\frac{1}{2}$-9}{9$\frac{1}{2}$-10-10}"/{20.5-21.5-23} {24-25.5-25.5} cm, ending by working Row 4.

Slip first {28-30-32}{34-38-40} sts onto st holder for right shoulder 3-needle bind off; slip next {36-37-38} {39-41-42} sts onto second st holder for neck; slip remaining {28-30-32}{34-38-40} sts onto third st holder for left shoulder 3-needle bind off; cut yarn.

LEFT FRONT

RIBBING

Cast on {50-52-55}{57-62-65} sts.

Work in K1, P1 ribbing for 2" (5 cm).

BODY

SIZES 32, 36, AND 42 ONLY

Row 1 (Right side)**:** P1, slip 1 as if to **knit**, K2, PSSO, ★ P2, slip 1 as if to **knit**, K2, PSSO; repeat from ★ across to last st, P1.

Row 2: K1, P1, YO, P1, ★ K2, P1, YO, P1; repeat from ★ across to last st, K1.

Row 3: P1, K3, (P2, K3) across to last st, P1.

Row 4: K1, P3, (K2, P3) across to last st, K1.

Repeat Rows 1-4 for pattern until Left Front measures same as Back to Armhole Shaping, ending by working a **wrong** side row.

SIZES 34, 38, AND 40 ONLY

Work in pattern same as Back until Left Front measures same as Back to Armhole Shaping, ending by working a **wrong** side row.

Note: Cardigan includes two edge stitches.

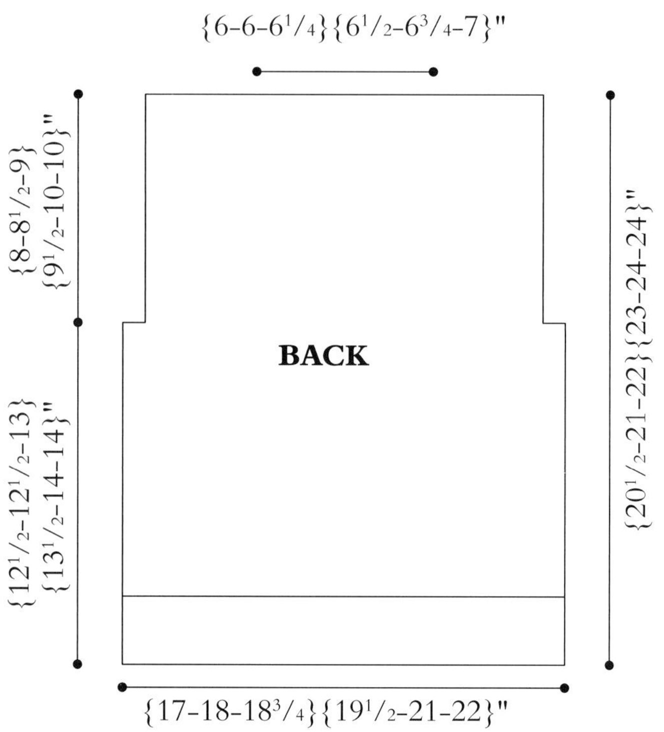

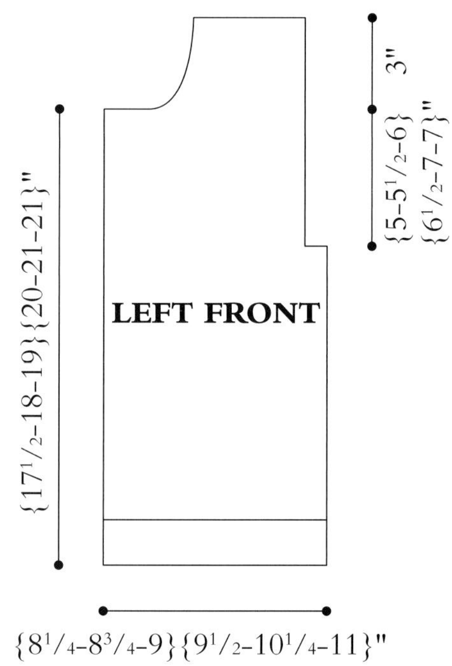

ARMHOLE SHAPING - ALL SIZES

Maintain established pattern throughout.

Row 1: Bind off 5 sts, work across: {45-47-50} {52-57-60} sts.

Work even until Armhole measures approximately {5-5$^{1}/_{2}$-6}{6$^{1}/_{2}$-7-7}"/{12.5-14-15}{16.5-18-18} cm, ending by working Row 3 of pattern.

NECK SHAPING

Row 1: Bind off {8-8-9}{9-10-11} sts, work across: {37-39-41}{43-47-49} sts.

Decrease one stitch at Neck edge on next row ***(see Decreases, pages 33 and 34)***, then decrease every other row, 8 times **more**; then work even for 2 rows: {28-30-32}{34-38-40} sts.

Slip Back left shoulder sts onto same size needle as Left Front.

Placing **right** sides together and using a larger size needle, join Back to Left Front at shoulder using the 3-needle bind off method ***(Fig. 13, page 34)***.

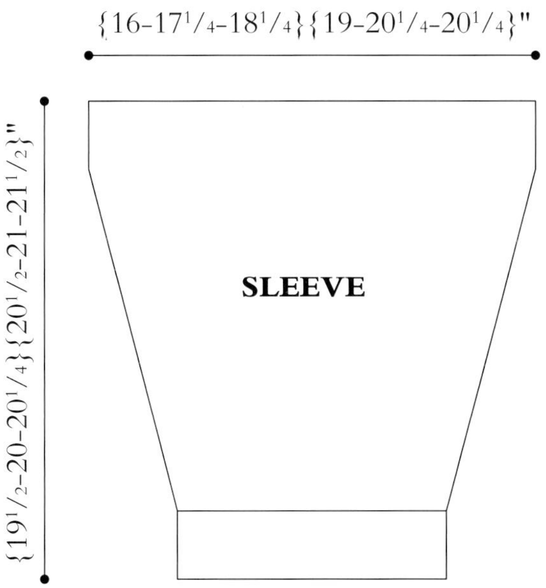

RIGHT FRONT

Work same as Left Front to Armhole Shaping, ending by working a **right** side row.

ARMHOLE SHAPING

Maintain established pattern throughout.

Row 1: Bind off 5 sts, work across: {45-47-50} {52-57-60} sts.

Work even until Armhole measures same as Left Front, ending by working Row 2 of pattern.

NECK SHAPING

Row 1: Bind off {8-8-9}{9-10-11} sts, work across: {37-39-41}{43-47-49} sts.

Decrease one stitch at Neck edge, every other **right** side row, 9 times; then work even for 2 rows: {28-30-32} {34-38-40} sts.

Slip Back right shoulder sts onto same size needle as Right Front.

Placing **right** sides together and using a larger size needle, join Back to Right Front at shoulder using the 3-needle bind off method.

SLEEVE (Make 2)

CUFF

Cast on {52-52-57}{57-57-57} sts.

Work in pattern same as Back Body for 18 rows.

Instructions continued on page 20.

BODY

Beginning with a **purl** row, work in Reverse Stockinette Stitch increasing one stitch at **each** edge ***(Figs. 4a & b, page 32)***, every fourth row, {0-0-0}{4-12-10} times ***(see Zeros, page 30)***; then increase every sixth row, {14-17-17}{15-10-12} times: {80-86-91} {95-101-101} sts.

Work even until Sleeve measures approximately {19$^{1}/_{2}$-20-20$^{1}/_{4}$}{20$^{1}/_{2}$-21-21$^{1}/_{2}$}"/{49.5-51-51.5} {52-53.5-54.5} cm from cast on edge **or** to desired length, ending by working a **knit** row.

Bind off all sts **loosely** in **purl**.

FINISHING

Sew Sleeves to sweater, placing center of Sleeve at shoulder seam.

Weave underarm and side in one continuous seam ***(Fig. 15, page 35)***.

NECK RIBBING

With **right** side facing, pick up {8-8-9}{9-10-11} sts across Right Front bound off sts ***(Figs. 14a & b, page 35)*** and 20 sts along neck edge, slip {36-37-38} {39-41-42} sts from Back st holder onto empty needle and knit across, pick up 20 sts along Right Front neck edge and {8-8-9}{9-10-11} sts across bound off sts: {92-93-96}{97-101-104} sts.

Work in K1, P1 ribbing for 4" (10 cm).

Bind off all sts **loosely**.

Sew zipper in place using sewing needle and thread.

Fold Neck Ribbing to **wrong** side and loosely sew bound off edge in place and sew along end of rows at neck edge, also enclosing the ends of the zipper tape.

Note: To prevent puckering, the rule of thumb is to pick up a stitch in 2 out of every 3 rows.

Enclose edge of zipper as follows:
With **wrong** side facing, pick up sts evenly along side edge of zipper.

Beginning with a **purl** row, work 3 rows in Stockinette Stitch.

Bind off all sts **loosely** in **knit**.

Using sewing needle and thread, sew flap over zipper tape thus enclosing the zipper.
Repeat on the other side of the zipper.

BLOCKING

Place the sweater on a flat surface and pin it to the finished bust measurement of the size that was made. Hold a steam iron or steamer just above the sweater and steam it thoroughly. Never let the weight of the iron touch your sweater because it will flatten the stitches. Leave the sweater pinned in place until it is completely dry.

something special

INTERMEDIATE

Simple lacework and a decorative bind-off makes this bolero fun to knit. For a feminine touch, form a simple pleat on each sleeve and finish it with a bow tie to create a baby doll look. It is sized for a very close fit.

Size	Finished Chest Measurement	
28-30	29"	(73.5 cm)
32-34	33"	(84 cm)
36-38	37"	(94 cm)
40-42	41"	(104 cm)
44-46	45"	(114.5 cm)

Size Note: Instructions are written with sizes 28-30 and 32-34 in the first set of braces { } and sizes 36-38, 40-42, and 44-46 in the second set. Instructions will be easier to read if you circle all the numbers pertaining to your size. If only one number is given, it applies to all sizes.

MATERIALS

Medium Weight Yarn
[2.1 ounces, 129 yards
(60 grams, 118 meters) per skein**]**:
{4-5}{5-6-7} skeins
Straight knitting needles, sizes 6 (4 mm) **and** 7 (4.5 mm) **or** sizes needed for gauge
36" (91.5 cm) Circular knitting needle, size 6 (4 mm)
Yarn needle

GAUGE: With larger size needles, in Eyelet pattern, 20 sts and 26 rows = 4" (10 cm)

Gauge Swatch: 5"w x 4"h (12.75 cm x 10 cm)
With larger size needles, cast on 25 sts.
Work same as Back Rows 1-26.
Bind off all sts.

BACK

With larger size straight needles, cast on {75-85}{95-105-115} sts.

Row 1 (Right side)**:** Knit across.

Row 2 AND ALL WRONG SIDE ROWS: Purl across.

Row 3: K5, K2 tog ***(Fig. 7, page 33)***, YO ***(Fig. 3a, page 32)***, K1, YO, **[**slip 1 as if to **knit**, K1, PSSO ***(Fig. 9, page 33)*****]**, K5, ★ K2 tog, YO, K1, YO, slip 1 as if to **knit**, K1, PSSO, K5; repeat from ★ across.

Row 5: Knit across.

Row 7: K3, YO, slip 1 as if to **knit**, K1, PSSO, K5, K2 tog, YO, ★ K1, YO, slip 1 as if to **knit**, K1, PSSO, K5, K2 tog, YO; repeat from ★ across to last 3 sts, K3.

Row 9: Knit across.

Repeat Rows 2-9 for Eyelet pattern until Back measures approximately {$6^1/_2$-7}{$7^1/_2$-8-8}"/{16.5-18}{19-20.5-20.5} cm from cast on edge, ending by working Row 4 or 8.

Instructions continued on page 22.

ARMHOLE SHAPING

Maintain established pattern throughout.

Rows 1 and 2: Bind off {3-5}{6-9-10} sts, work across: {69-75}{83-87-95} sts.

If there aren't enough sts to work the pattern decrease in addition to the armhole decrease, then don't work the last YO.

Row 3 (Decrease row)**:** K1, slip 1 as if to **knit**, K1, PSSO, work across to last 3 sts, K2 tog, K1: {67-73}{81-85-93} sts.

Row 4: Purl across.

Repeat Rows 3 and 4, {2-3}{4-5-6} times: {63-67}{73-75-81} sts.

Work even until Armholes measure approximately {7 1/2-8}{8-8 1/2-9}"/{19-20.5}{20.5-21.5-23} cm, ending by working a **wrong** side row.

SHOULDER SHAPING

Rows 1-4: Bind off {6-7}{8-8-9} sts, work across: {39-39}{41-43-45} sts.

Rows 5 and 6: Bind off {7-7}{7-8-9} sts, work across: {25-25}{27-27-27} sts.

Bind off remaining sts.

LEFT FRONT

With larger size straight needles, cast on {75-85}{95-105-115} sts.

Rows 1-9: Work in Eyelet pattern same as Back.

Row 10: Bind off {38-43}{48-53-58} sts for tie, purl across: {37-42}{47-52-57} sts.

Row 11 (Decrease row)**:** Work across in pattern to last 3 sts, K2 tog, K1: {36-41}{46-51-56} sts.

Maintaining pattern, continue to decrease one stitch at neck edge in same manner, every sixth row, {11-11}{12-12-12} times **more** AND AT THE SAME TIME when Left Front measures same as Back to Armhole Shaping and ending by working Row 4 or 8, bind off {3-5}{6-9-10} stitches at beginning of next row, then decrease one stitch at Armhole edge every other row, {3-4}{5-6-7} times: {19-21}{23-24-27} sts.

Work even until Left Front measures same as Back to Shoulder Shaping, ending by working a **purl** row.

SHOULDER SHAPING

Row 1: Bind off {6-7}{8-8-9} sts, work across: {13-14}{15-16-18} sts.

Row 2: Work across.

Rows 3 and 4: Repeat Rows 1 and 2: {7-7}{7-8-9} sts.

Bind off remaining sts.

Instructions continued on page 24.

RIGHT FRONT

With larger size straight needles, cast on {75-85}{95-105-115} sts.

Rows 1-10: Work in Eyelet pattern same as Back.

Row 11: Bind off {38-43}{48-53-58} sts for tie, work across in pattern: {37-42}{47-52-57} sts.

Row 12: Purl across.

Row 13 (Decrease row)**:** K1, slip 1 as if to **knit**, K1, PSSO, work across in pattern: {36-41}{46-51-56} sts.

Maintaining pattern, continue to decrease one stitch at neck edge in same manner, every sixth row, {11-11}{12-12-12} times **more** AND AT THE SAME TIME when Right Front measures same as Back to Armhole Shaping and ending by working Row 5 or 9, bind off {3-5}{6-9-10} stitches at beginning of next row, then decrease one stitch at Armhole edge every other row, {3-4}{5-6-7} times: {19-21}{23-24-27} sts.

Work even until Right Front measures same as Back to Shoulder Shaping, ending by working a **right** side row.

SHOULDER SHAPING

Work same as Left Front.

SLEEVE (Make 2)

With larger size straight needles, cast on {75-75}{85-95-95} sts.

Rows 1-8: Work in Eyelet pattern same as Back.

CAP SHAPING

Maintain established pattern throughout.

Rows 1 and 2: Bind off {3-5}{6-9-10} sts, work across: {69-65}{73-77-75} sts.

Row 3 (Decrease row)**:** K1, slip 1 as if to **knit**, K1, PSSO, work across to last 3 sts, K2 tog, K1: {67-63}{71-75-73} sts.

Row 4: Purl across.

Rows 5 thru {19-27}{27-33-35}: Repeat Rows 3 and 4, {7-11}{11-14-15} times; then repeat Row 3 once **more**: {51-39}{47-45-41} sts.

Note: Bolero includes two edge stitches.

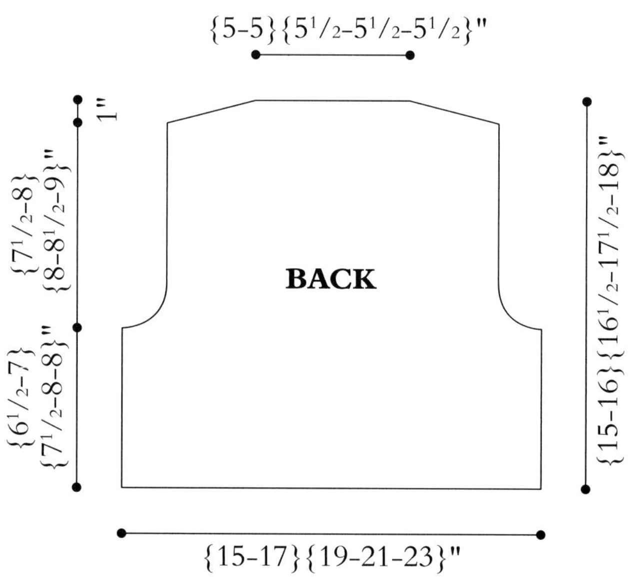

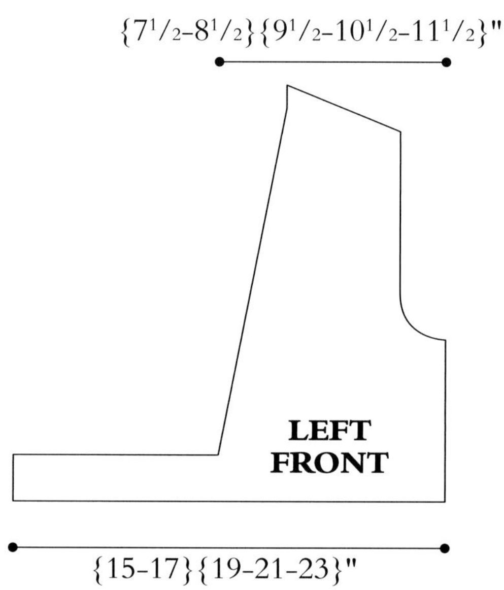

Row {20-28}{28-34-36} (Decrease row)**:** P1, P2 tog ***(Fig. 11, page 34)***, purl across to last 3 sts, SSP ***(Fig. 12, page 34)***, P1: {49-37}{45-43-39} sts.

Continue to decrease one stitch at **each** edge, every row, {12-6}{10-8-6} times **more**: {25-25}{25-27-27} sts.

Next 4 Rows: Bind off 3 sts, work across: {13-13}{13-15-15} sts.

Bind off remaining sts.

EDGING

With **right** side facing and using smaller size straight needles, pick up {75-75}{85-95-95} sts evenly spaced along Sleeve cast on edge ***(Figs. 14a & b, page 35)***.

Row 1: Purl across.

Row 2 (Bind off row)**:** Bind off 2 sts, ★ slip st from right needle back onto left needle, add on 2 sts ***(Figs. 2a & b, page 31)***, bind off 4 sts; repeat from ★ until all sts have been bound off.

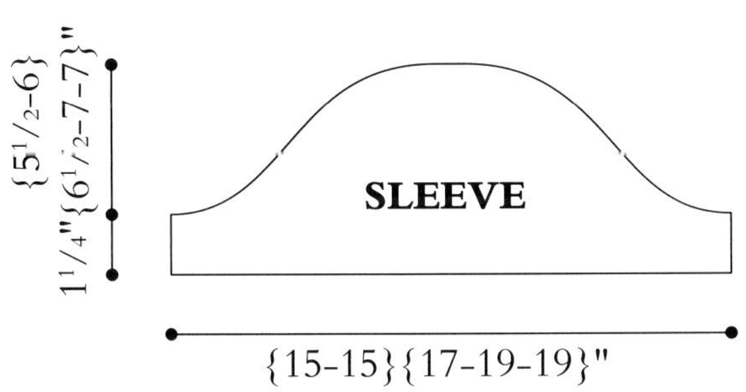

FINISHING

For Sleeve darts, fold Sleeve in half and place markers 2" (5 cm) from cast on edge, 1" (2.5 cm) from each side of fold. With **right** side facing and using a long length of yarn, sew through each marked st, joining them together; tie in a bow.

Repeat for second Sleeve.

Sew shoulder seams.

Sew Sleeves to sweater, placing center of Sleeve Cap at shoulder seam and matching bound off sts.

Weave underarm and side in one continuous seam ***(Fig. 15, page 35)***.

NECK EDGING

With **right** side facing, using circular needle and beginning on Right Front above tie, pick up an even number of sts evenly along Right Front edge, pick up {25-25}{27-27-27} sts across Back neck edge, pick up an even number of sts evenly along Left Front edge.

Row 1: Purl across.

Bind off Row: Work same as for Sleeves.

BODY EDGING

With **right** side facing and using circular needle, pick up an odd number of sts across bottom edge of sweater, working between ties.

Row 1: Purl across.

Bind off Row: Work same as for Sleeves.

basically beautiful

INTERMEDIATE

Shown on back cover.

The long ribbing on the waist and sleeves creates a slimming effect. Increases are worked at the bust to nicely contour the sweater to your curves. This is an indispensable garment for any wardrobe!

Size	Finished Chest Measurement	
32	32"	(81.5 cm)
34	34 1/2"	(87.5 cm)
36	36"	(91.5 cm)
38	38 1/2"	(98 cm)
40	40"	(101.5 cm)
42	42 1/2"	(108 cm)

Size Note: Instructions are written with sizes 32, 34, and 36 in the first set of braces { } and sizes 38, 40, and 42 in the second set of braces. Instructions will be easier to read if you circle all the numbers pertaining to your size. If only one number is given, it applies to all sizes.

MATERIALS

LIGHT 3

Light Weight Yarn
[1.75 ounces, 192 yards (50 grams, 175 meters) per hank]:
{5-6-6}{7-7-8} hanks

Straight knitting needles, size 6 (4 mm) **or** size needed for gauge

Note: You will need a third needle to work the 3-needle bind off. One size larger than needles used to achieve gauge will work best.

Stitch holders - 2

Markers - 2

Yarn needle

GAUGE: In Stockinette Stitch,
24 sts and 32 rows = 4" (10 cm)

STITCH GUIDE

M1 LEFT

Insert the **left** needle under the horizontal strand between the stitches from the **front**. Then knit into the **back** of the strand ***(Figs. 5a & b, page 32)***.

M1 RIGHT

Insert the **left** needle under the horizontal strand between the stitches from the **back**. Then knit into the **front** of the strand ***(Figs. 6a & b, page 32)***.

BACK

BODY RIBBING

Cast on {82-90-94}{102-106-114} sts.

Row 1: P2, (K2, P2) across.

Row 2 (Right side)**:** K2, (P2, K2) across.

Repeat Rows 1 and 2 for 10" (25.5 cm), ending by working Row 1.

BODICE

Row 1: Knit across increasing 16 sts evenly spaced ***(Figs. 4a & b, page 32)***: {98-106-110}{118-122-130} sts.

Beginning with a **purl** row, work in Stockinette Stitch until Back measures approximately {14-14-14}{14 1/2-14 1/2-15}"/{35.5-35.5-35.5}{37-37-38} cm from cast on edge, ending by working a **purl** row.

ARMHOLE SHAPING

Rows 1 and 2: Bind off {6-7-7}{8-9-10} sts, work across: {86-92-96}{102-104-110} sts.

Row 3 (Decrease row)**:** K1, SSK ***(Figs. 8a-c, page 33)***, knit across to last 3 sts, K2 tog ***(Fig. 7, page 33)***, K1: {84-90-94}{100-102-108} sts.

Decrease one stitch at **each** edge in same manner, every other row, {4-5-5}{6-6-8} times **more**: {76-80-84}{88-90-92} sts.

Work even until Armholes measure approximately {7½-7½-8}{8½-9-9½}"/{19-19-20.5}{21.5-23-24} cm, ending by working a **purl** row.

NECK SHAPING

Both sides of Neck are worked at the same time using separate yarn for **each** side.

Note: It takes two stitches to bind off the first stitch.

Row 1: Knit {13-15-16}{18-17-18} sts, bind off center {50-50-52}{52-56-56} sts; with second yarn, knit across: {13-15-16}{18-17-18} sts **each** side.

Row 2: Purl across to within 2 sts of Neck edge, SSP ***(Fig. 12, page 34)***; with second yarn, P2 tog ***(Fig. 11, page 34)***, purl across: {12-14-15}{17-16-17} sts **each** side.

Row 3: Knit across to within 2 sts of Neck edge, K2 tog; with second yarn, SSK, knit across: {11-13-14}{16-15-16} sts **each** side.

Slip remaining sts onto 2 separate st holders for 3-needle bind off; cut yarns.

Instructions continued on page 28.

Note: Sweater includes two edge stitches.

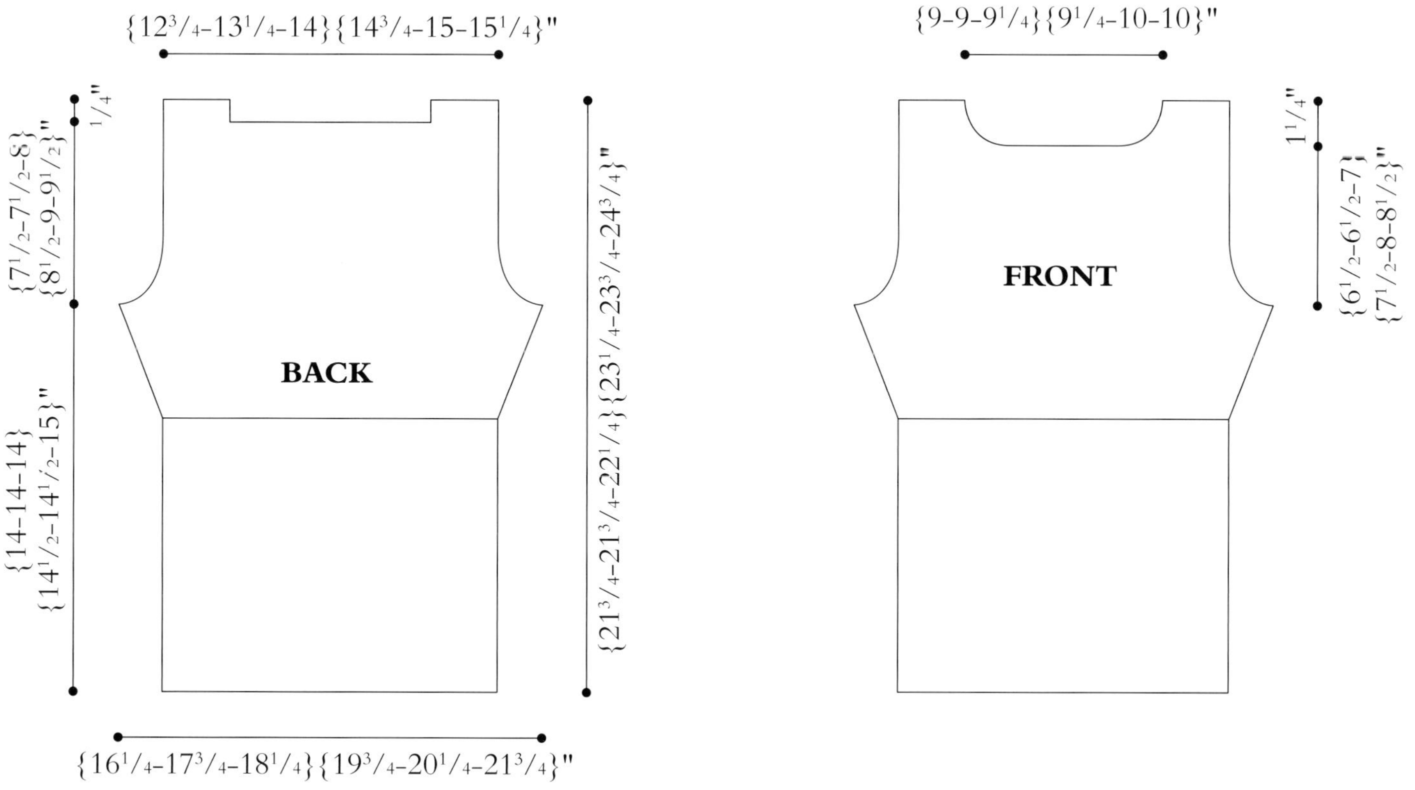

FRONT

BODY RIBBING

Work same as Back.

BODICE

Row 1: Knit across.

Row 2: Purl {27-30-31}{34-35-38} sts, place marker for dart placement ***(see Markers, page 30)***, purl {28-30-32}{34-36-38} sts, place marker, purl across.

Row 3 (Increase row)**:** ★ Knit across to within one st of marker, M1 left, K2, M1 right; repeat from ★ once **more**, knit across: {86-94-98}{106-110-118} sts.

Work in Stockinette Stitch, increasing in same manner as Row 3, every fourth row, 3 times **more**: {98-106-110}{118-122-130} sts.

Work even until Front measures same as Back to Armhole Shaping, ending by working a **purl** row.

ARMHOLE SHAPING

Work same as Back until Armholes measure approximately {6 1/2-6 1/2-7}{7 1/2-8-8 1/2}"/ {16.5-16.5-18}{19-20.5-21.5} cm, ending by working a **purl** row: {76-80-84}{88-90-92} sts.

NECK SHAPING

Both sides of Neck are worked at the same time using separate yarn for **each** side.

Row 1: Knit {19-21-22}{24-23-24} sts, bind off center {38-38-40}{40-44-44} sts; with second yarn, knit across: {19-21-22}{24-23-24} sts **each** side.

Row 2 (Decrease row)**:** Purl across to within 2 sts of Neck edge, SSP; with second yarn, P2 tog, purl across: {18-20-21}{23-22-23} sts **each** side.

Row 3 (Decrease row)**:** Knit across to within 2 sts of Neck edge, K2 tog; with second yarn, SSK, knit across: {17-19-20}{22-21-22} sts **each** side.

Rows 4-9: Repeat Rows 2 and 3, 3 times: {11-13-14} {16-15-16} sts **each** side.

Row 10: Purl across.

Slip Back left shoulder sts onto same size needle as Front.

Placing **right** sides together and using a larger size needle, join Front to Back at left shoulder using the 3-needle bind off method ***(Fig. 13, page 34)***.

Join Front to Back at right shoulder in same manner.

SLEEVE (Make 2)

RIBBING

Cast on {50-50-50}{54-54-58} sts.

Row 1: P2, (K2, P2) across.

Row 2 (Right side)**:** K2, (P2, K2) across.

Repeat Rows 1 and 2 for 5" (12.5 cm), ending by working Row 1.

BODY

Beginning with a **knit** row, work in Stockinette Stitch, increasing one stitch at **each** edge ***(Figs. 4a & b, page 32)***, every other row, {0-0-0}{0-6-6} times ***(see Zeros, page 30)***; then increase every fourth row, {7-16-23}{24-21-22} times; then increase every sixth row, {10-4-0}{0-0-0} times: {84-90-96} {102-108-114} sts.

Work even until Sleeve measures approximately {17-17-17$^{1}/_{2}$}{18-18-18$^{1}/_{2}$}"/{43-43-44.5} {45.5-45.5-47} cm from cast on edge **or** desired length to underarm, ending by working a **purl** row.

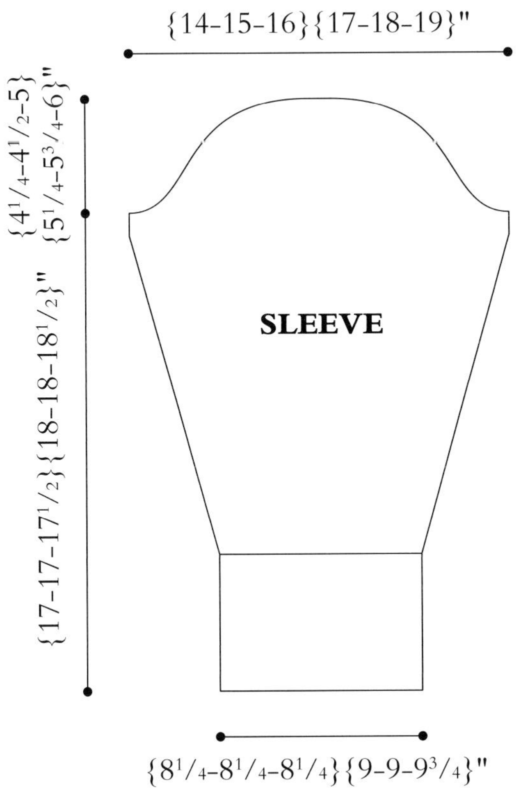

CAP SHAPING

Rows 1 and 2: Bind off {6-7-7}{8-9-10} sts, work across: {72-76-82}{86-90-94} sts.

Row 3 (Decrease row)**:** K1, SSK, knit across to last 3 sts, K2 tog, K1: {70-74-80}{84-88-92} sts.

Continue to decrease one stitch at **each** edge, every other row, {6-6-9}{10-12-12} times **more**; then decrease every row, {16-17-15}{15-15-16} times: {26-28-32}{34-34-36} sts.

Next 4 Rows: Bind off {3-3-4}{4-4-4} sts, work across: {14-16-16}{18-18-20} sts.

Bind off remaining sts.

FINISHING

Sew Sleeves to sweater, placing center of Sleeve Cap at shoulder seam and matching bound off sts.

Weave underarm and side in one continuous seam ***(Fig. 15, page 35)***.

NECK EDGING

With **right** side facing and beginning at Back neck edge, (pick up one st and slip it onto the left needle, then knit the st) twice ***(Figs. 14a & b, page 35)***, pass the first st on right needle over the second st to bind off, ★ pick up one st and slip it onto the left needle, then knit the st, pass the first st on right needle over the second st; repeat from ★ around entire neck edge; cut yarn and pull end through loop.

general information

ABBREVIATIONS

cm	centimeters
K	knit
M1	make one
mm	millimeters
P	purl
PSSO	pass slipped stitch over
Rnd(s)	Round(s)
SSK	slip, slip, knit
SSP	slip, slip, purl
st(s)	stitch(es)
tbl	through back loop(s)
tog	together
YO	yarn over

★ — work instructions following ★ as many **more** times as indicated in addition to the first time.

( ) or **[ ]** — work enclosed instructions **as many** times as specified by the number immediately following **or** contains explanatory remarks.

colon (:) — the number(s) given after a colon at the end of a row or round denote(s) the number of stitches you should have on that row or round.

work even — work without increasing or decreasing in the established pattern.

GAUGE

Exact gauge is **essential** for proper fit. Before beginning your sweater, make a sample swatch in the yarn and needle specified in the individual instructions. After completing the swatch, measure it, counting your stitches and rows carefully. If your swatch is larger or smaller than specified, **make another, changing needle size to get the correct gauge**. Keep trying until you find the size needles that will give you the specified gauge.

MARKERS

As a convenience to you, we have used markers to help distinguish the beginning of a pattern or round, or to mark placement of increases or decreases. Place markers as instructed. You may use purchased markers or tie a length of contrasting color yarn around the needle. When you reach a marker on each row or round, slip it from the left needle to the right needle; remove it when no longer needed.

ZEROS

To consolidate the length of an involved pattern, zeros are sometimes used so that all sizes can be combined. For example, increase every sixth row 5{1-0} time(s) means the first size would increase 5 times, the second size would increase once, and the largest size would do nothing.

KNIT TERMINOLOGY		
UNITED STATES		**INTERNATIONAL**
gauge	=	tension
bind off	=	cast off
yarn over (YO)	=	yarn forward (yfwd) **or** yarn around needle (yrn)

BEGINNER	Projects for first-time knitters using basic knit and purl stitches. Minimal shaping.
EASY	Projects using basic stitches, repetitive stitch patterns, simple color changes, and simple shaping and finishing.
INTERMEDIATE	Projects with a variety of stitches, such as basic cables and lace, simple intarsia, double-pointed needles and knitting in the round needle techniques, mid-level shaping and finishing.
EXPERIENCED	Projects using advanced techniques and stitches, such as short rows, fair isle, more intricate intarsia, cables, lace patterns, and numerous color changes.

KNIT ONE THROUGH BACK LOOP *(abbreviated K1 tbl)*

Insert the right needle into the **back** of the next stitch from **front** to **back** ***(Fig. 1)***, then **knit** the stitch.

Fig. 1

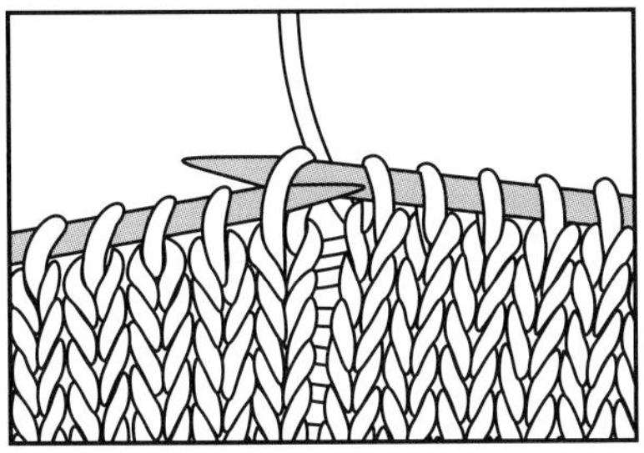

ADDING NEW STITCHES

Insert the right needle into stitch as if to **knit**, yarn over and pull loop through ***(Fig. 2a)***, insert the left needle into the loop just worked from **front** to **back** and slip the loop onto the left needle ***(Fig. 2b)***. Repeat for required number of stitches.

Fig. 2a

Fig. 2b

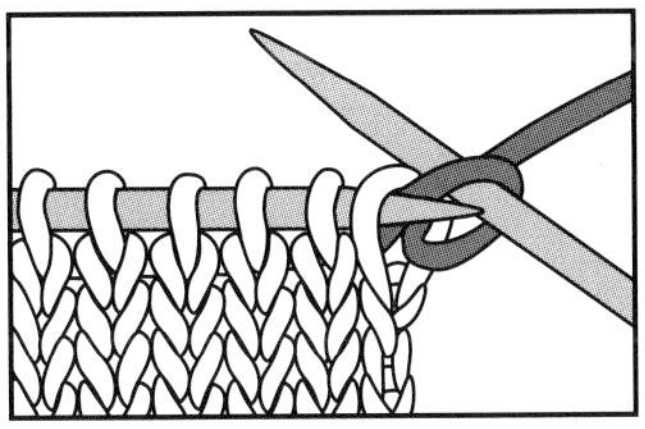

KNITTING NEEDLES		
UNITED STATES	ENGLISH U.K.	METRIC (mm)
0	13	2
1	12	2.25
2	11	2.75
3	10	3.25
4	9	3.5
5	8	3.75
6	7	4
7	6	4.5
8	5	5
9	4	5.5
10	3	6
10½	2	6.5
11	1	8
13	00	9
15	000	10
17	---	12.75

Yarn Weight Symbol & Names	LACE 0	SUPER FINE 1	FINE 2	LIGHT 3	MEDIUM 4	BULKY 5	SUPER BULKY 6
Type of Yarns in Category	Fingering, size 10 crochet thread	Sock, Fingering, Baby	Sport, Baby	DK, Light Worsted	Worsted, Afghan, Aran	Chunky, Craft, Rug	Bulky, Roving
Knit Gauge Range* in Stockinette St to 4" (10 cm)	33-40** sts	27-32 sts	23-26 sts	21-24 sts	16-20 sts	12-15 sts	6-11 sts
Advised Needle Size Range	000-1	1 to 3	3 to 5	5 to 7	7 to 9	9 to 11	11 and larger

*GUIDELINES ONLY: The chart above reflects the most commonly used gauges and needle sizes for specific yarn categories.

** Lace weight yarns are usually knitted on larger needles to create lacy openwork patterns. Accordingly, a gauge range is difficult to determine. Always follow the gauge stated in your pattern.

YARN OVERS *(abbreviated YO)*

After a knit stitch, before a knit stitch

Bring the yarn forward **between** the needles, then back **over** the top of the right hand needle, so that it is now in position to knit the next stitch ***(Fig. 3a)***.

After a purl stitch, before a purl stitch

Take the yarn **over** the right hand needle to the back, then forward **under** it, so that it is now in position to purl the next stitch ***(Fig. 3b)***.

Fig. 3a

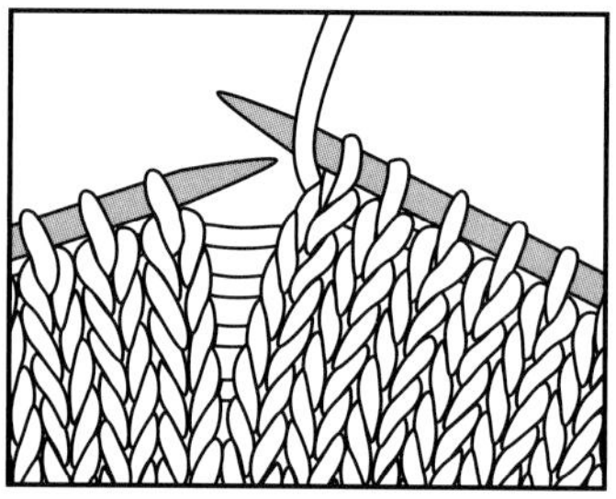

Fig. 3b

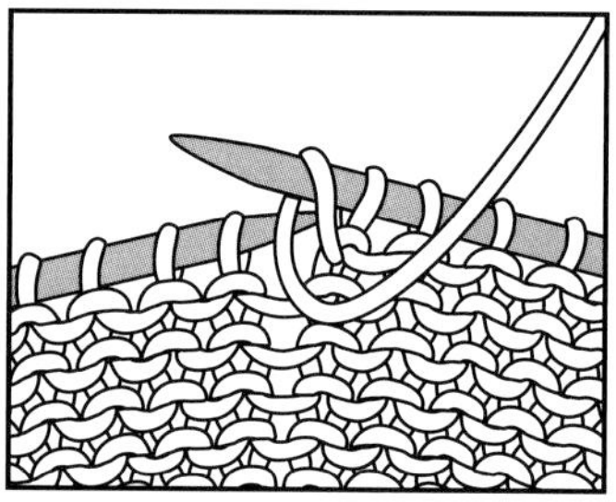

KNIT INCREASE

Knit the next stitch but do **not** slip the old stitch off the left needle ***(Fig. 4a)***. Insert the right needle into the **back** loop of the **same** stitch and knit it ***(Fig. 4b)***, then slip the old stitch off the left needle.

Fig. 4a

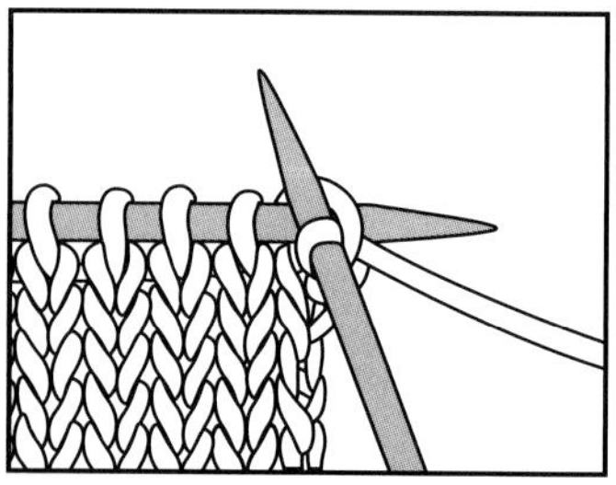

Fig. 4b

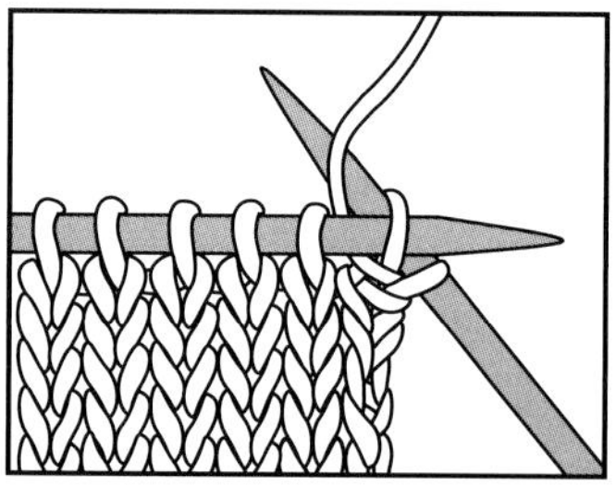

MAKE ONE LEFT *(abbreviated M1 left)*

Insert the **left** needle under the horizontal strand between the stitches from the **front** ***(Fig. 5a)***. Then knit into the **back** of the strand ***(Fig. 5b)***.

Fig. 5a

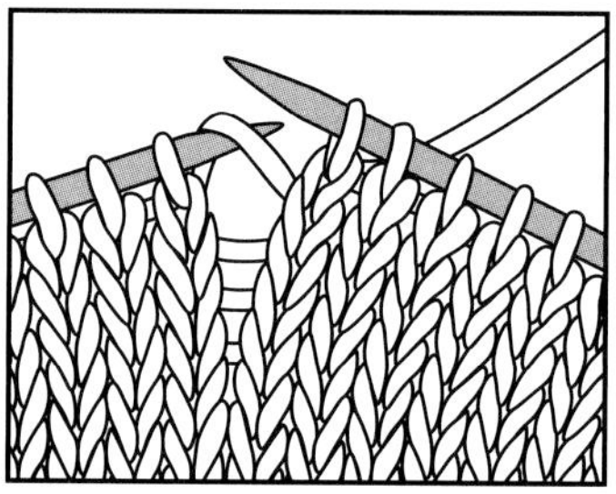

Fig. 5b

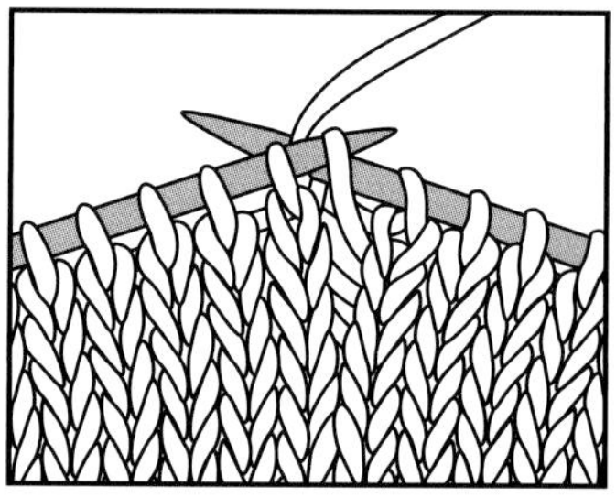

MAKE ONE RIGHT

(abbreviated M1 right)

Insert the **left** needle under the horizontal strand between the stitches from the **back** ***(Fig. 6a)***. Then knit into the **front** of the strand ***(Fig. 6b)***.

Fig. 6a

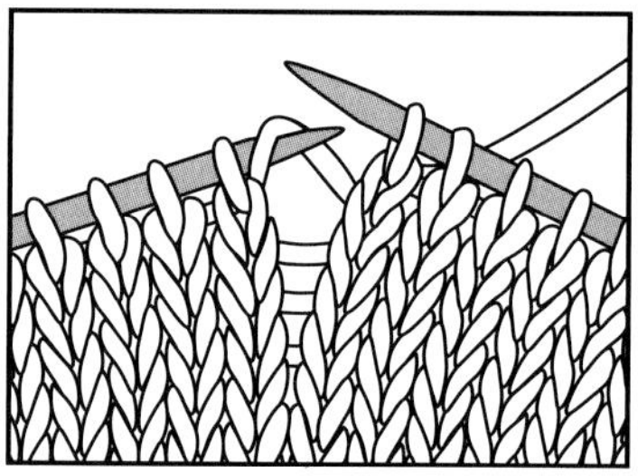

Fig. 6b

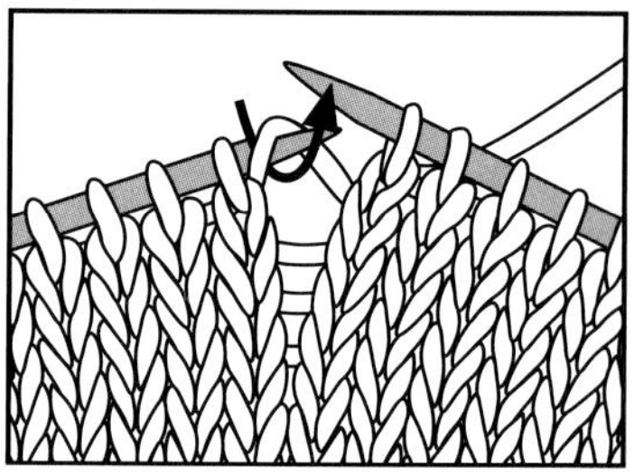

DECREASES

KNIT 2 TOGETHER *(abbreviated K2 tog)*

Insert the right needle into the **front** of the first two stitches on the left needle as if to **knit** ***(Fig. 7)***, then **knit** them together as if they were one stitch.

Fig. 7

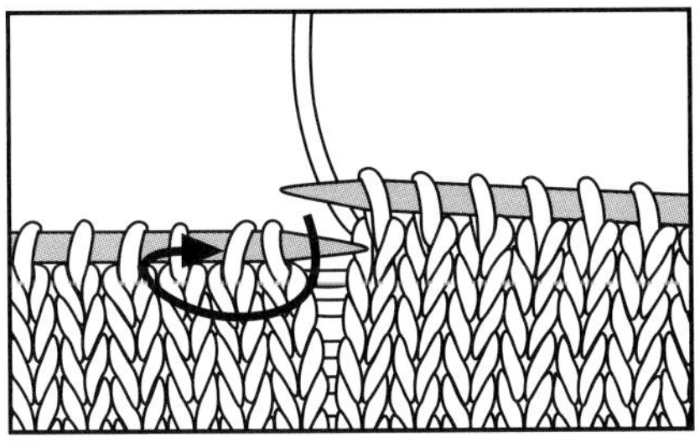

SLIP, SLIP, KNIT *(abbreviated SSK)*

Separately slip two stitches as if to **knit** ***(Fig. 8a)***. Insert the **left** needle into the **front** of both slipped stitches ***(Fig. 8b)*** and then **knit** them together as if they were one stitch ***(Fig. 8c)***.

Fig. 8a

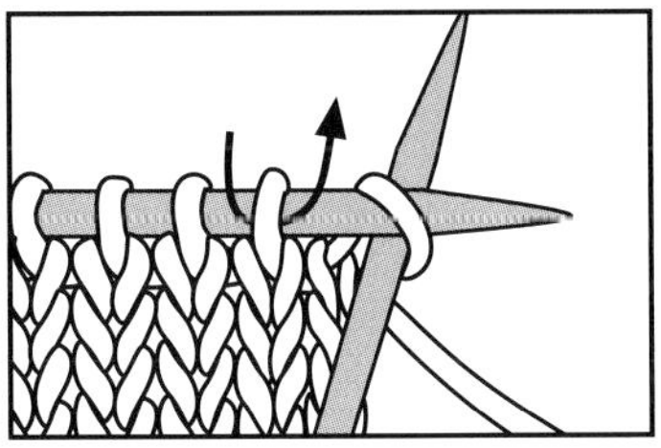

Fig. 8b

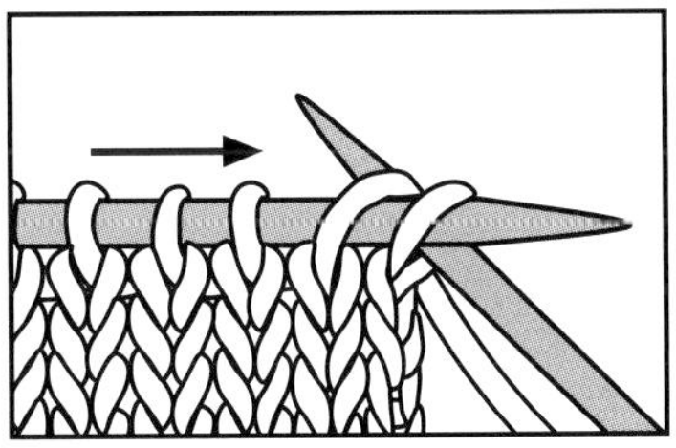

Fig. 8c

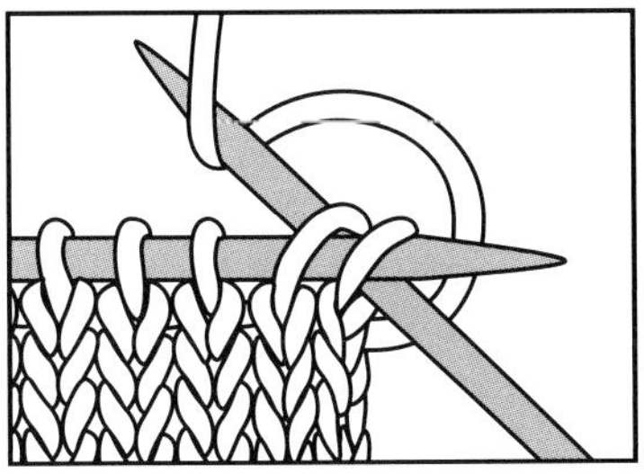

SLIP 1, KNIT 1, PASS SLIPPED STITCH OVER *(abbreviated slip 1, K1, PSSO)*

Slip one stitch as if to **knit**. Knit the next stitch. With the left needle, bring the slipped stitch over the knit stitch ***(Fig. 9)*** and off the needle.

Fig. 9

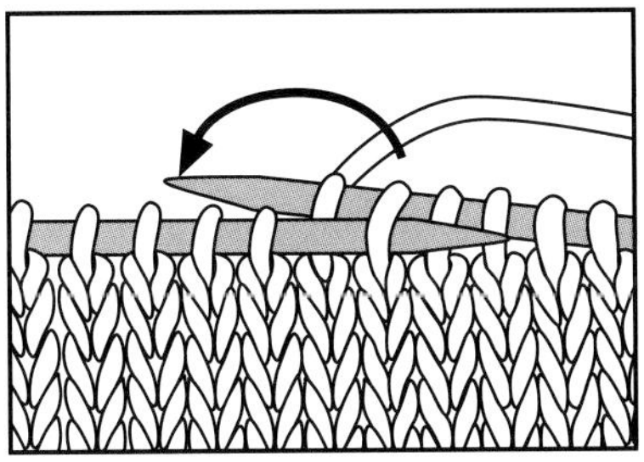

SLIP 1, KNIT 2, PASS SLIPPED STITCH OVER *(abbreviated slip 1, K2, PSSO)*

Slip one stitch as if to **knit**. Knit the next two stitches. With the left needle, bring the slipped stitch over the two knit stitches ***(Fig. 10)*** and off the needle.

Fig. 10

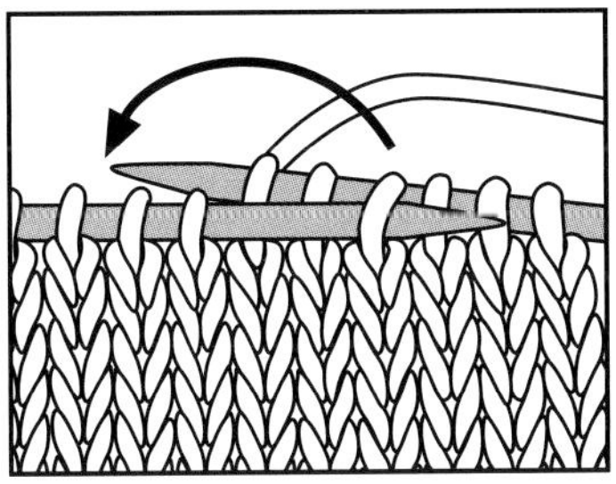

PURL 2 TOGETHER *(abbreviated P2 tog)*

Insert the right needle into the **front** of the first two stitches on the left needle as if to **purl** ***(Fig. 11)***, then **purl** them together as if they were one stitch.

Fig. 11

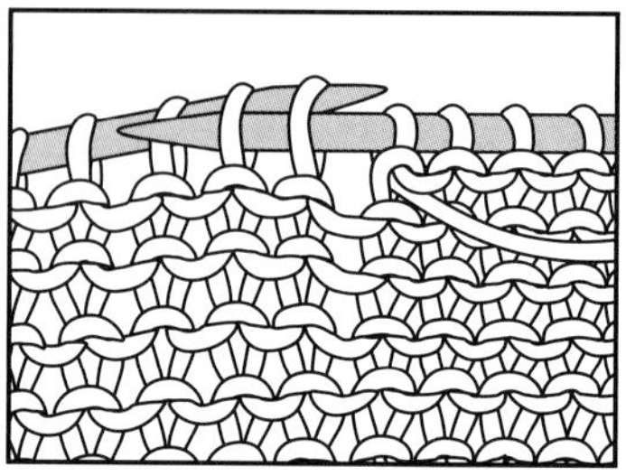

SLIP, SLIP, PURL *(abbreviated SSP)*

Separately slip two stitches as if to **knit**. Place these two stitches back onto the left needle. Insert the right needle into the **back** of both stitches from **back** to **front** ***(Fig. 12)*** and purl them together.

Fig. 12

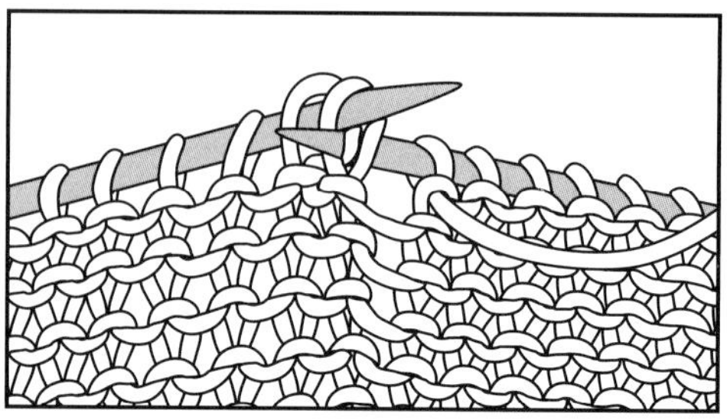

3-NEEDLE BIND OFF

Holding pieces with needles parallel to each other, insert a third needle as if to **knit** into the first stitch on the front needle **and** into the first stitch on the back needle ***(Fig. 13)***. Knit these two stitches together and slip them off the needle. ★ Knit the next stitch on each needle together and slip them off the needle. To bind off, insert one of the left needles into the first stitch on the right needle and pull the first stitch over the second stitch and off the right needle; repeat from ★ across until all of the shoulder or ruffle stitches have been bound off.

Fig. 13

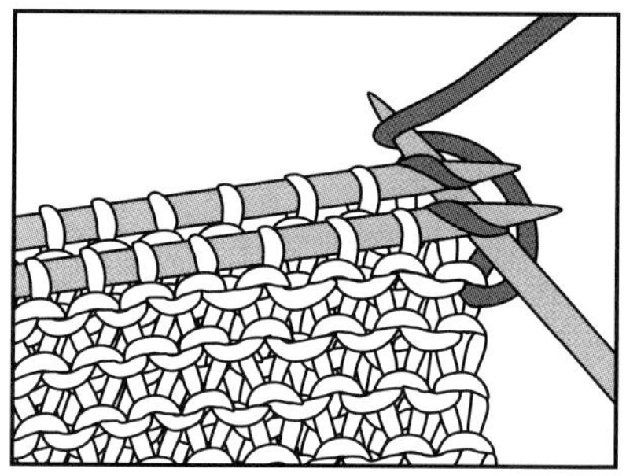

PICKING UP STITCHES

When instructed to pick up stitches, insert the needle from the **front** to the **back** under two strands at the edge of the worked piece ***(Figs. 14a & b)***. Put the yarn around the needle as if to **knit**, then bring the needle with the yarn back through the stitch to the right side, resulting in a stitch on the needle.

Repeat this along the edge, picking up the required number of stitches.

A crochet hook may be helpful to pull yarn through.

Fig. 14a

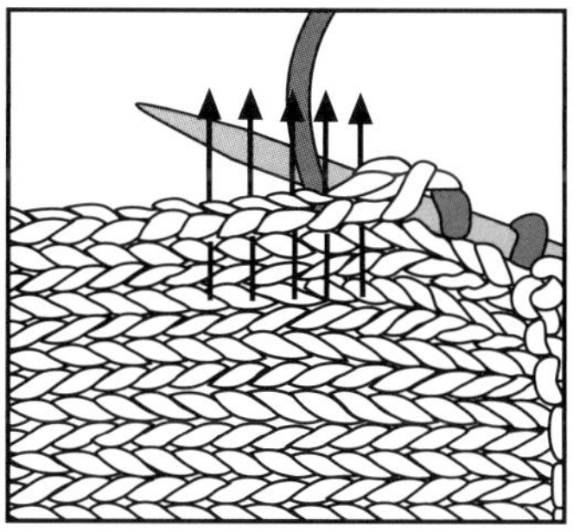

Fig. 14b

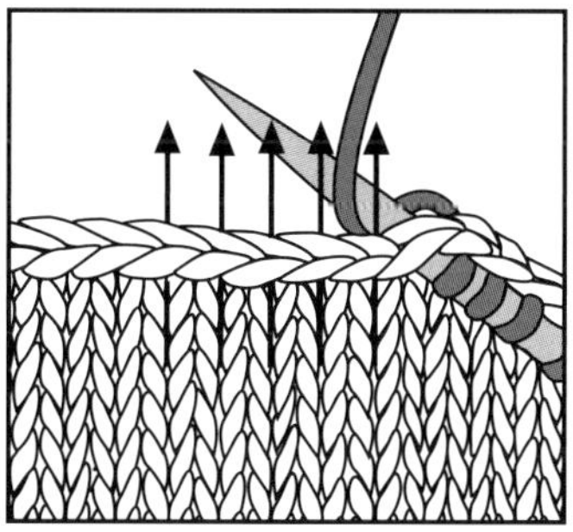

WEAVING SEAMS

With the **right** side of both pieces facing you and edges even, sew through both sides once to secure the seam. Insert the needle under the bar **between** the first and second stitches on the row and pull the yarn through ***(Fig. 15)***. Insert the needle under the next bar on the second side. Repeat from side to side, being careful to match rows. If the edges are different lengths, it may be necessary to insert the needle under two bars at one edge.

Fig. 15

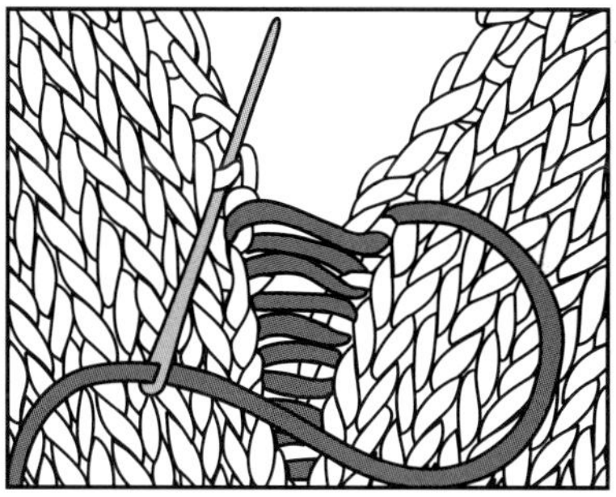

YARN INFORMATION

The items in this leaflet were made using a variety of yarns. Any brand of the specified weight of yarn may be used. It is best to refer to the yardage/meters when determining how many balls, skeins, or hanks to purchase. Remember, to achieve the same look, it is the weight of yarn that is important, not the brand of yarn.

For your convenience, listed below are the specific yarns used to create our photography models.

FEMININE FRILLS
Bernat® Satin
#04307 Sultana Raisin

JUST ENOUGH
Cascade Yarns Pastaza
#076 Orange

LIGHT LACE-UP
Lion Brand® Microspun
Pink - #146 Fuchsia
Brown - #126 Coffee
Lion Brand® Incredible
#206 Autumn Leaves

PLENTY OF ZIP
Patons® Classic Wool Merino
#00230 Bright Red

SOMETHING SPECIAL
Bernat® Cot'n Corn
#19128 Water

BASICALLY BEAUTIFUL
Elsebeth Lavold Silky Wool
#053 Bronzed Green

We have made every effort to ensure that these instructions are accurate and complete. We cannot, however, be responsible for human error, typographical mistakes, or variations in individual work.

Production Team: Instructional Writer/Editor - Cathy Hardy; Editorial Writer - Susan McManus Johnson; Senior Graphic Artist - Lora Puls; Graphic Artists - Jacob Casleton, Katherine Laughlin, and Janie Wright; Photo Stylist - Cora Brown; and Photographer - Jason Masters.

Instructions tested and photo models made by Sue Galucki and Margaret Taverner.